THIS CANDLEWICK BIOGRAPHY BELONGS TO:

For Kristen Nobles

CROSSING NIAGARA

The Death-Defying Tightrope Adventures of the Great Blondin

Matt Tavares

CANDLEWICK PRESS

First edition in this format 2018

Library of Congress Catalog Card Number 2014957109

ISBN 978-0-7636-6823-5 (hardcover)
ISBN 978-1-5362-0341-7 (reformatted hardcover)
ISBN 978-1-5362-0342-4 (reformatted paperback)

18 19 20 21 22 23 APS 10 9 8 7 6 5 4 3 2 1

Printed in Humen, Dongguan, China

This book was typeset in Dolly.
The illustrations were done in watercolor, gouache, and pencil.

Candlewick Press
99 Dover Street
Somerville, Massachusetts 02144

visit us at www.candlewick.com

TABLE OF CONTENTS

— Chapter One —

When Jean François Gravelet was just five years old, he gave his first public performance as a tightrope walker. People were amazed.

Before long, he was the greatest tightrope walker in the whole world. They called him the Great Blondin.

As he got older, Blondin loved being in the circus, but he yearned for more. He wanted to do something amazing, something impossible, something that had never been done before.

Then one day, Blondin's circus troupe visited Niagara Falls. As soon as he saw it, he exclaimed, "What a splendid place to bridge with a tightrope!" The other acrobats laughed.

But Blondin was not joking.

Right away, Blondin set out to make this dream happen. He visited the office of the local newspaper, the *Daily Gazette*, and told the reporters about his plan.

They all thought Blondin was crazy! But a story about a madman trying to cross Niagara Falls on a tightrope was sure to sell lots of newspapers. The owners of the *Daily Gazette* pledged their full support.

Blondin wanted to stretch his rope directly over Horseshoe Falls, from Goat Island on one side to Canada on the other. It was the most majestic, and the most dangerous, part of Niagara Falls.

But the owner of Goat Island, General Porter, would not allow it. He thought that anyone who attempted to cross Niagara Falls on a tightrope faced certain death. And he wanted no part of it.

Blondin instead secured his rope a bit downriver from the falls, in a park called White's Pleasure Grounds. The owner, Mr. White, fenced off a large section of the park and charged visitors twenty-five cents to watch Blondin make his crossing, splitting the profits fifty-fifty with Blondin. The landowner on the Canadian side allowed Blondin to use his land without asking for any money at all.

The rope was more than eleven hundred feet long and just three inches wide. It hung one hundred and sixty feet above the raging Niagara River. Dozens of smaller ropes, called "guy ropes," supported it and kept it steady. Blondin insisted on crawling out onto the rope and attaching every guy rope himself.

← Chapter Two →

The first spectators arrived early in the morning. By late afternoon, the cliffs were packed with people. They came on steamships from Toronto, on overcrowded trains from Buffalo, and in horse-drawn carriages from every direction.

They all came to see the Great Blondin.

Some doubted whether Blondin would even show up. Some expected to watch him plummet to his death. Gamblers bet large amounts of money on how it would end.

The odds were not in Blondin's favor.

Then, just after five o'clock, he appeared, accompanied by his manager, Harry Colcord. A roar rose from the crowd.

Blondin stepped onto the rope and chatted with the spectators. He asked if anyone would like to volunteer to ride on his back. Everyone laughed. Blondin shrugged, then waved his hand and a brass band began to play.

Then he started walking.

CHAPTER THREE

THE CROWD FELL SILENT, but Blondin was not afraid. He had practiced all his life for this. One step at a time, he walked. The rope felt as wide as a bridge.

A quarter of the way across, Blondin stopped. The crowd held its breath. Perhaps something had gone wrong!

And then Blondin began a series of amazing tricks.
With each trick, the crowd cheered louder,

and louder,

and louder!

Blondin smiled to himself, then jumped up and walked faster.

Halfway across, he stopped again. He pulled a ball of twine from his pocket and tossed one end down to the water below, where the little steamship, *Maid of the Mist,* was passing beneath him. A friend on the ship tied a bottle to the twine.

Blondin pulled the bottle up, raised it in a toast to the people on both sides of the river, and took a big gulp. Then he walked even faster, all the way to the Canadian side.

— CHAPTER FOUR —

BLONDIN HAD DONE IT: Something amazing! Something
impossible! Something that had never been done before! Then, just
when everyone thought this spectacular, once-in-a-lifetime event had
come to an end . . . he stepped back onto the rope, and he did it again.

He walked all the way back across to America.

The crowd lifted him up onto their shoulders and carried him to a horse-drawn carriage. The brass band played "Yankee Doodle" as Blondin was paraded through town.

At the end of the parade, Blondin announced that he would cross Niagara again, on the Fourth of July. The air echoed with cheers of delight.

News of Blondin's remarkable feat spread quickly around the world, but many were skeptical. Some newspaper articles claimed that the whole thing had never happened. Thousands of people decided to go to Niagara, to see for themselves.

On the Fourth of July, Blondin was back. Again, he asked if anyone would like to ride across on his back. Again, everybody laughed. Blondin shrugged.

He was determined to make this performance even more amazing than the first. So this time, he walked all the way across—blindfolded!

CHAPTER FIVE

DURING THE SUMMERS OF 1859 AND 1860, Blondin performed
on his rope more than a dozen times. With each performance, he
tried to do something even more amazing, even more impossible,
something that had never, ever been done before.

It seemed that Blondin had done it all. But there was one thing that would top everything he had done so far. He told the *Daily Gazette* that for his next performance, he would cross Niagara Falls with a man on his back. His manager, Harry Colcord, was ecstatic! This was sure to attract the biggest crowd yet! But, he wondered, who was this brave soul who had volunteered to ride on Blondin's back?

CHAPTER SIX

WHEN THE DAY FINALLY ARRIVED, the cliffs were more crowded than ever, just as Blondin had hoped. Blondin cleared his throat and announced the name of his passenger.

"Harry Colcord!" he exclaimed.

Harry laughed, but then he realized that Blondin wasn't joking. His face turned pale. Blondin was crazy! But then he thought about it. He had attended every performance so far, and he had seen all the amazing things that Blondin could do on a tightrope. He knew that Blondin could do this, too. Harry agreed to do it.

"If I sway, sway with me," said Blondin. "Do not attempt to do any balancing yourself. If you do, we will both go to our death."

And then Blondin started walking.

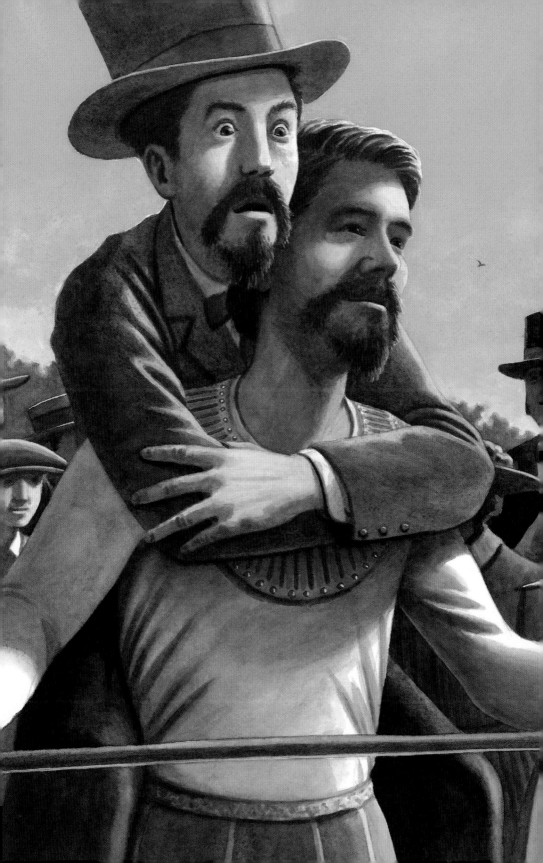

It turned out to be more difficult than Blondin had expected. He had to stop seven times to catch his breath. Then, halfway across, Blondin started to lose his balance. Harry Colcord held on tight and tried not to look down.

Blondin ran about thirty feet to a more stable part of the tightrope, but the guy rope holding it steady snapped!

He ran for the next guy rope and just barely made it.

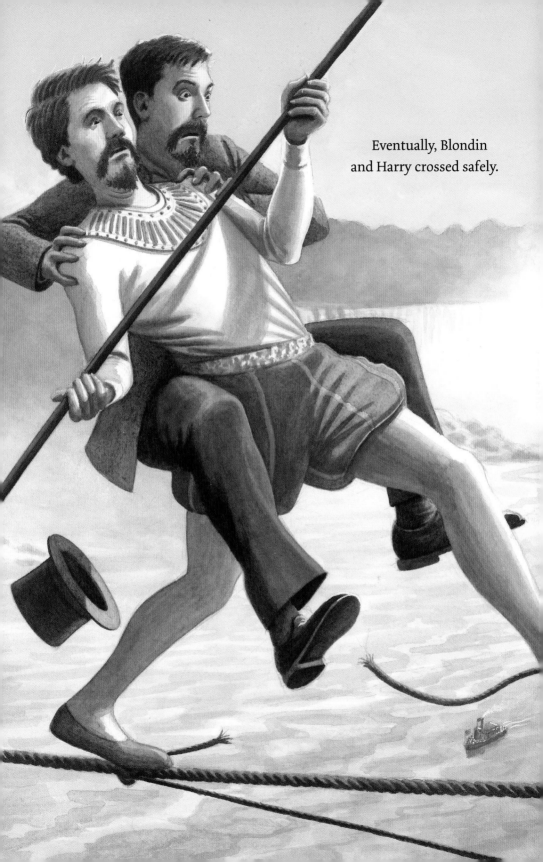

Eventually, Blondin and Harry crossed safely.

━ Chapter Seven ━

By the end of summer 1860, Blondin crossing Niagara on a tightrope was no longer front-page news. The trains to Niagara Falls were no longer crowded. From his rope, Blondin could barely even hear the cheers.

Then, one crisp September evening, Blondin gave his greatest performance yet. He repeated all the tricks he had done before, in one amazing show. Harry Colcord even volunteered to ride on his back again—and this time, they made it all the way across without stopping once.

When Blondin stepped down from his rope, he smiled to himself. He had done everything he had set out to do. He had done something amazing, something impossible, something that had never been done before. He had done it over and over again. And now it was time for something new.

So he left Niagara Falls, and he never returned.

Author's Note

Soon after I started working on this book, I visited Niagara Falls with my family. It was awe-inspiring to see it up close, to stand next to the falls and soak in (literally) the sheer massiveness of it. We got drenched on the *Maid of the Mist* and ventured out to the end of the observation platform at Prospect Point. I tried to imagine what it must have felt like for Blondin to be right near that very spot, unthinkably high above the raging river, walking on a rope just three inches wide (it was scary enough standing on a twenty-foot-wide platform)!

The most common question people asked me while I was working on this book was, "Did he ever fall?" The answer, incredibly, is no. After leaving Niagara Falls in September 1860, Blondin spent the next two decades traveling the world, performing on his tightrope. He gave his final public performance at the age of seventy-two. Amazingly, in over sixty-five years as a rope walker, he was never injured. After stepping down from the rope for the final time, he retired to a villa in England. He called it Niagara Villa.

Acknowledgments

Thanks to the helpful staff of the Niagara Falls Public Library in Niagara Falls, New York, who kindly prepared for my visit by filling a library book cart with hundreds of Blondin-related articles, which made my job so much easier. And special thanks to Spencer, Zachary, and Travis Carpenter; Sarah, Ava, and Molly Tavares; Katie Cunningham, Hayley Parker, Kristen Nobles, and Rosemary Stimola.

➤ SELECTED BIBLIOGRAPHY ➤

Banks, George Linnaeus. *Blondin: His Life and Performances*. London: Routledge, Warne, and Routledge, 1862.

Graham, Lloyd. "Blondin, the Hero of Niagara." *American Heritage*, August 1958.

Lockport (NY) Journal and Courier. "The Great Feat Performed; Walking the Gorge of Niagara River on a Tight-Rope! THE THING IS DID!" July 1, 1859, p. 2.

New York Daily Tribune. "M. Blondin's Tight-rope Feat." July 1, 1859, p. 5.

New York Times. "An Exciting Scene: M. Blondin's Feat at Niagara Falls." July 4, 1859.

———. "The Prince at Niagara: Visit to the Falls." September 17, 1860.

Niagara (NY) Daily Gazette. "The Great Feat Performed—Mons. Blondin Triumphant—He Walks Across Niagara River on a Tight Rope— Great Excitement Among the Spectators." July 1, 1859, p. 3.

———. "Mons. Blondin Performs a Daring Feat; The Spectators Astonished!!" June 24, 1859, p. 3.

———. "Mons. Blondin—Today." June 30, 1859, p. 1.

Otago (New Zealand) Witness. "A Visit to the Chevalier Blondin's Home." January 1885, p. 26.

Price, John B. "Some Details of the Life and Exploits of Blondin, the Rope-Walker." Paper for the Union des Historiens du Cirque, 1958.

Salem (MA) Observer. "Blondin on the Tight Rope." July 9, 1859, p. 1.

Wilson, Ken. *Everybody's Heard of Blondin*. Kent, UK: Pond View Books, 1990.

Index

MATT TAVARES is the author-illustrator of *Henry Aaron's Dream*, *There Goes Ted Williams*, *Becoming Babe Ruth,* and *Growing Up Pedro*, as well as *Zachary's Ball*, *Oliver's Game*, *Mudball*, and *Red and Lulu*. He is the illustrator of *'Twas the Night Before Christmas*, *Over the River and Through the Wood*, *Lady Liberty* by Doreen Rappaport, *The Gingerbread Pirates* by Kristin Kladstrup, *Jubilee!* by Alicia Potter, and *Lighter than Air* by Matthew Clark Smith. Matt Tavares lives in Ogunquit, Maine.